What's Inside Me?
My Stomach

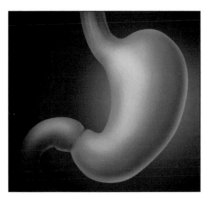

Dana Meachen Rau

Benchmark Books

MARSHALL CAVENDISH
NEW YORK

My Stomach

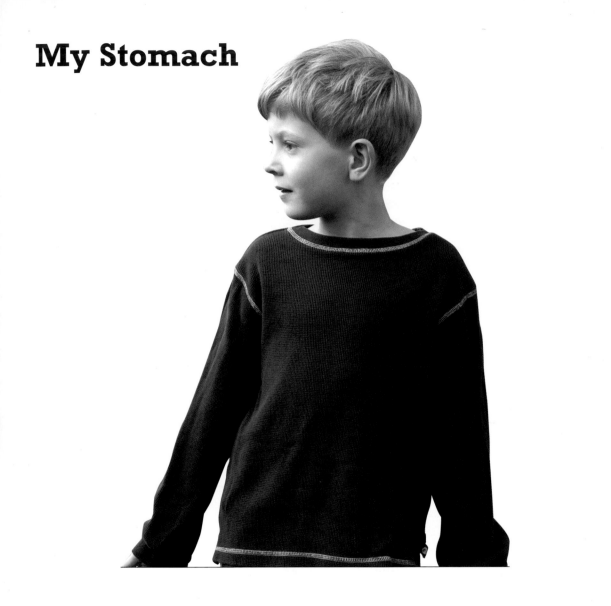

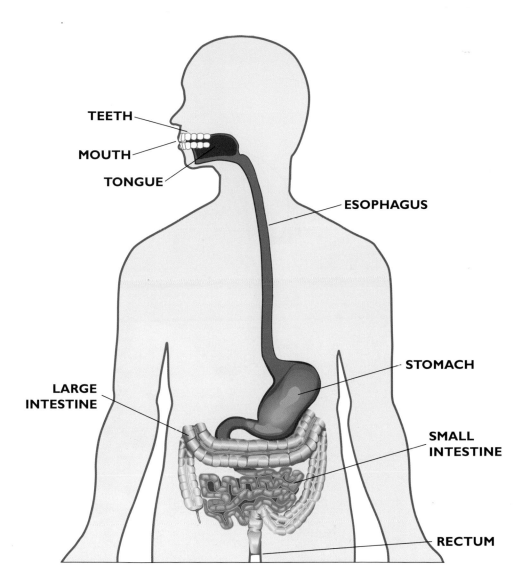

TEETH

MOUTH

TONGUE

ESOPHAGUS

STOMACH

LARGE INTESTINE

SMALL INTESTINE

RECTUM

993

3

What did you bring for lunch today? Peanut butter on wheat bread is yummy. Carrots are crunchy. Milk is a healthy drink.

Your body needs food to grow.
Food gives your body *energy*.

Food keeps you strong and healthy.

You eat food every day. It goes into your mouth. *Waste* from your food comes out of your body when you go to the bathroom.

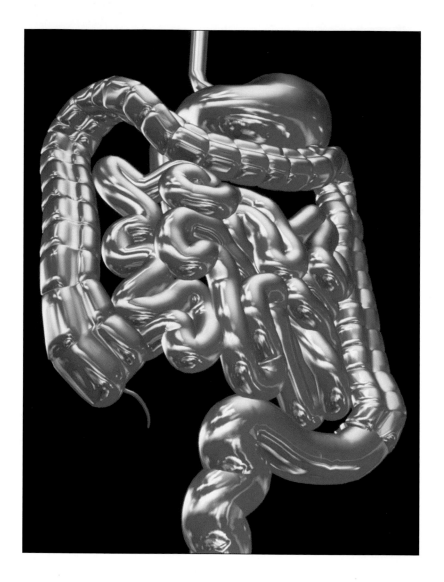

10

But what happens to the food while it is inside you?

Food travels a long path through your body. This path is called the *digestive system*.

Your stomach is an important part of your digestive system. It turns food into *nutrients*. Nutrients are used by all parts of your body.

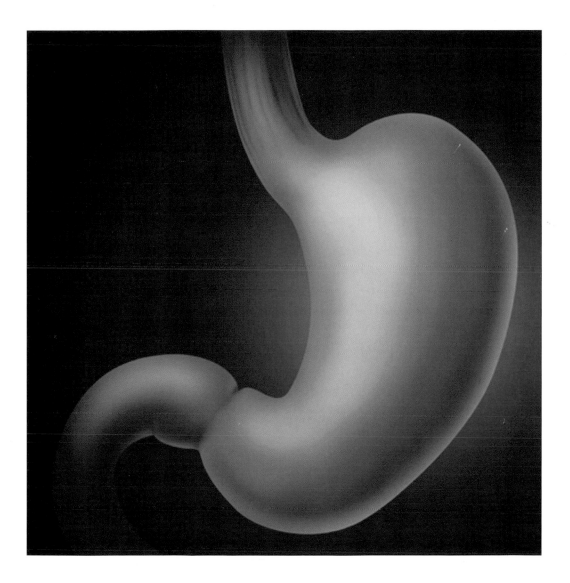

13

You put food in your mouth. Your teeth chew your food. *Saliva*, or spit, mixes with food and makes it soft.

Next, you *swallow*. Your tongue pushes the food to the back of your throat.

The food travels down a tube called the *esophagus*. The tube leads into your stomach.

Your stomach is like a bag. It holds the food.

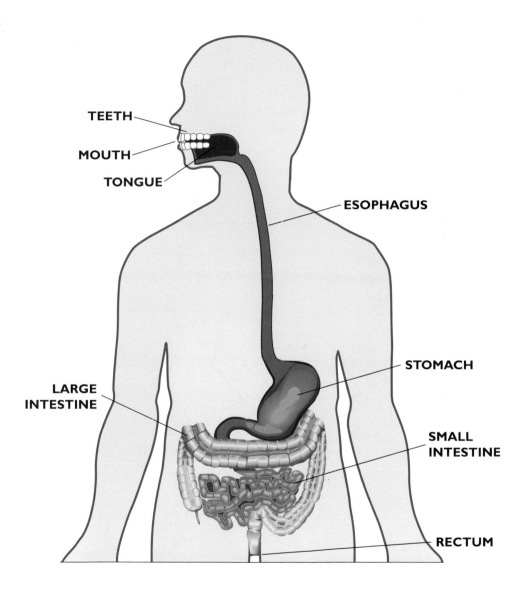

TEETH

MOUTH

TONGUE

ESOPHAGUS

STOMACH

LARGE
INTESTINE

SMALL
INTESTINE

RECTUM

17

The inside of your stomach is bumpy. Your stomach stretches bigger and bigger as you eat more food.

You feel full when you have a lot of food in your stomach.

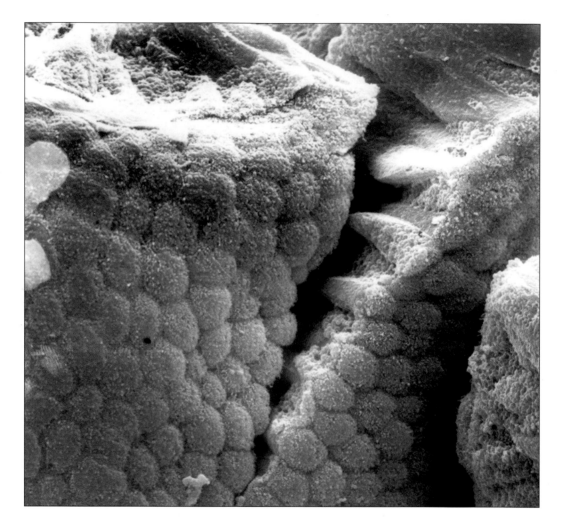

Inside the stomach

Your stomach is very strong. It moves around to mush up food into small pieces. Juices in your stomach make the food very soft.

The food is filled with nutrients. It becomes thick and soupy.

Food stays in your stomach for about three hours. Then your stomach pushes the food into another tube. It is called the *small intestine*.

The small intestine is very long and thin. It winds around inside your body.

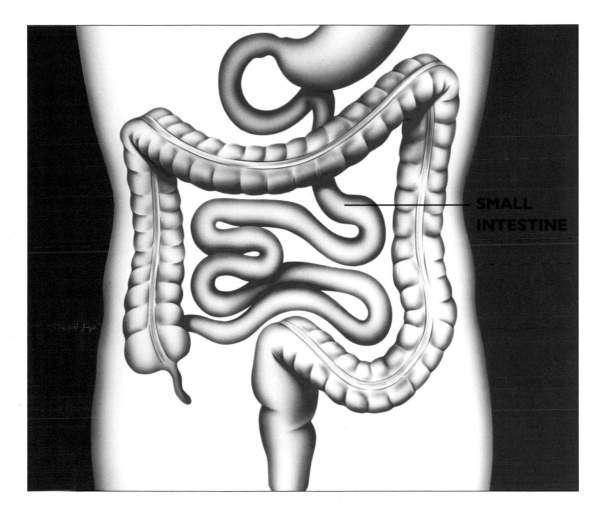

SMALL
INTESTINE

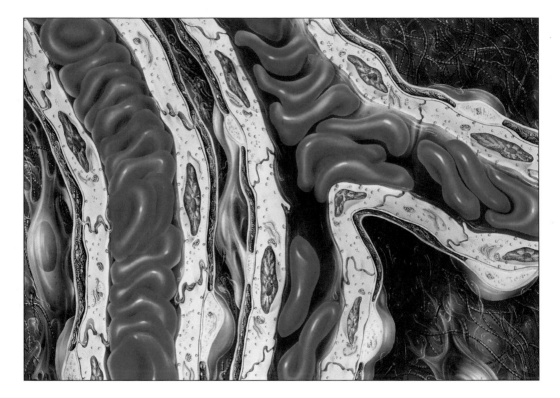

Blood traveling through the body

From the small intestine, the nutrients go into your blood.

Blood travels all around your body. It carries the nutrients to parts of your body that need them.

The small intestine leads to another tube. It is called the *large intestine*.

The large intestine gets rid of the food your body does not need. Waste travels through the large intestine to your *rectum*. Then the waste leaves your body through an opening.

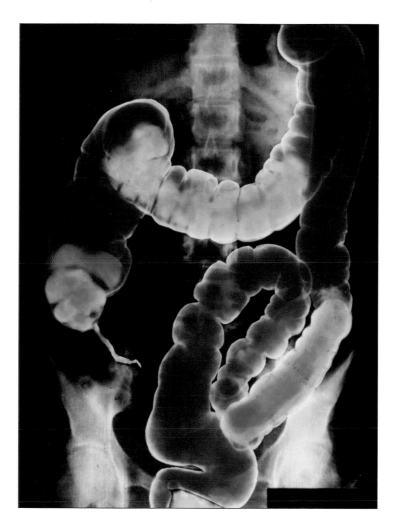

X-ray of the large intestine

You need to eat good food
every day.

Healthy food gives you a
healthy body.

Challenge Words

digestive system (die-JES-tiv SIS-tuhm)—The path food travels through your body.

energy (EN-uhr-jee)—What your body needs to be active.

esophagus (i-SOF-uh-guhs)—The tube that leads from your mouth to your stomach.

large intestine (large in-TES-tin)—The tube that leads from your small intestine to your rectum.

nutrients (NEW-tree-uhnts)—The parts of food your body needs to stay healthy.

rectum (rek-TUM)—The end of your large intestine.

saliva (suh-LIE-vuh)—The watery juice in your mouth that makes food soft.

small intestine (small in-TES-tin)—The long tube that sends nutrients into the blood.

swallow—To move food from your mouth into your esophagus.

waste—The parts of food your body does not need.

Index

Page numbers in **boldface** are illustrations.

With thanks to Nanci Vargus, Ed.D.
and Beth Walker Gambro, reading consultants

Benchmark Books
Marshall Cavendish
99 White Plains Road
Tarrytown, New York 10591-9001
www.marshallcavendish.com

Library of Congress Cataloging-in-Publication Data

Rau, Dana Meachen, 1971–
My stomach / by Dana Meachen Rau.
p. cm. — (Bookworms: What's inside me?)
Includes index.
ISBN 0-7614-1782-6
1. Stomach—Juvenile literature. 2. Gastrointestinal system—Juvenile literature. 3. Digestion—Juvenile literature.
I. Title. II. Series.

QP151.R38 2004
612.3—dc22
2004003057

Photo Research by Anne Burns Images

Cover Photo by Corbis: Royalty Free

The photographs in this book are used with permission and through the courtesy of:
Custom Medical Stock Photo: pp. 1, 13, 20. Jay Mallin: p. 2. Corbis: p. 4 Charles Gupton; p. 6 Bob Winsett; p. 7 David H. Wells; p. 9 Norbert Schaefer; p. 14 Richard Gross; p. 18 Christoph Wilhelm; p. 28 LWA-Sharie Kennedy; p. 28 Ed Bock. Photo Researchers: p. 10 Alfred Pasieka; p. 23 John Bavosi; p. 24 Medical Art Service; p. 27 CNRI.

Series design by Becky Terhune

Printed in China
1 3 5 6 4 2